TURNING INSIDE OUT

TURNING
INSIDE
OUT

poems by
Sandra
Kolankiewicz

Black Lawrence Press
New York

Black Lawrence Press
www.blacklawrence.com

Executive Editor: Diane Goettel
Book Design: Steven Seighman

Black Lawrence Press
115 Center Ave.
Aspinwall, PA 15215
U.S.A.

Published 2009 by Black Lawrence Press, a division of Dzanc Books

First edition 2009
ISBN: 9780982622803

Printed in the United States

Contents

For Edgar Whan

The New Me

I'll begin by not lying.
That would be a good start—

to be clear as a drop of sea water
in spite of its salt,

not like a rock in the harbor which guides
at low tide, scuttles at high,

that part of the landscape people just accept,
steer around even when they forget where it is.

But where to go from there,
which isn't the same as telling the truth?

Smoking will be second.
I'll no longer have to say

the butts aren't mine, that I didn't crush them—
there, right next to the steps—while I was waiting,

twisted little stubs on the spalling concrete,
bleeding thin brown in the rain.

Not pointing my breasts at other
women's husbands will come next.

Then, I'll lay the snickering and my old guffaw aside
the lies, the cigarettes, and the hard nipples

pressing through the thin shirt. Most likely
thoughtless comments will be the last to go.

How does one remember to be kind
when someone else finds the lover,

buys the house, has the baby, picks the winner,
gets the job, self nominates for the award?

When I have grounded my little boat until high tide, or
if I've really botched it, beached myself until

planks on the hull can be replaced,
and I have to find someone else to help me,

someone I won't be able to pay for awhile?
When a lie, a cigarette, or a breast

will just as easily do, and no will ever know
except me?

Keeping Pigeons

If you knew about having to keep the loft,
how they need perches, baths, enriched feed,
fresh water twice a day or else they weaken,
would you ever get started?
If you had been warned that the bright
feather speckles on those white grizzled chests,
the product of all that breeding,
would forestall vacations,
sometimes bring disease,
or that raising them would fall under threat of regulation,
even become forbidden,
against the law in some places,
like Chicago

Or if you realized that when you moved to a different house,
they could never again be allowed to fly.
They would get lost,
unable to learn a new home,
forever in search of that one coop only,
the one where they were imprinted
by your hand, as if just that first feeding,
and no other care you could later give them,
were more important than any new place chosen by you,
some place where you might wish to live one day,
perhaps alone

If you understood then that with pigeons a new coop can never do.
You will have to bring them with you when you go,
prisoners in your aviary, the biggest you can afford,

to which you will transport them in a wire box:
they won't fly there on their own.

Or if you knew you could be cruel
and the birds would still return.
Or that in order to train them,
you would have to rise three hours early,
make your way out into the country,
then let them go by tossing them into the air
to be driven home by their inertial
routing, some inner mechanism
registering the experience of the journey
so that they can retrace it;
flying by sign, sight, landmarks:
churches, bodies of water, urban parks;
using smells, sounds, sonar, their magnetic sense
through these times of such breaking apart, brought back always
by their love of the loft.

Based on an article by Susan Orlean, "Little Wing," *The New Yorker*, Feb 13 & 20, 2006

Intelligent Design

We emerge from the sea in the moonlight,
sand firm under our feet.
With each rising step the water uncovers our eyes, mouths,
throats, our breasts,
the seaweed in our fingers.

Waves nudge the backs of our knees,
roll past us,
melt into foam on the sand, drawn back
to begin a slow turn once again.

Our voices on the beach are
full of the bones
we are not supposed to have.

Yva

When I first met them, I wanted
nothing to do with them:
they made my teeth peel.
Though they were important
in some literary way,
I never answered their post.
Yva was different.
She always liked a leg up.
She was ready for that sort of thing;
they had money.

They had a garden, too, which everyone
also whispered about,
though most had never seen it.
What kind of soil, what kind of fertilizer
makes delphinium six feet tall
and foxglove thick as grape clusters?

Yva would meet them for lunch in that garden,
pushing open their front door,
clicking through their wide hall, stepping out
into the sunlight where they smoked easily around a set table:
fresh watercress and endive
turned out prettily on the plates
before the fish was served.
There were bowls of lemon water, she said,
to dip their fingers in later.

They separately seduced her, days apart,
each on the same bench before the overwhelming wisteria,
both of them comparing the size and arrangement
of the fleshy blooms to the pendulous breasts
of many-breasted Hindu goddesses.

But where were the servants? I asked,
shocked, thinking of all the windows,
Yva splayed, the purple aroma,
the sound of insistent bees,
my own skin tingling.

She'd already met the kitchen girl, she said,
paid her from the start to bring their writing papers to the garden
while they were napping
so she could read about herself,
even what would eventually be scratched out.

Later, in her own letters
to her own intimates,
she would claim to have been the rope
they pulled back and forth
to inspire their work.
She had been the reason for the gun.

The Necessity of Photographs

Here, this is her,
trying to untie the scratchy bow on an Easter bonnet,
scowling out between the fat
arms of a grandmother.

The other children in the background
are caught, forever at play,
soon to be separated from her
by a frozen wood where they
will stand shivering and small while she
runs on toward their burnt-out house
to be sure it is true.

Women have always stopped to bury their man,
even when corn needs harvesting
and ears hang ripe,
heavy on the stalk.
Grief becomes a black dress then,
packed in the closet when the thing is over,
before the fields
begin to rot.

John 8, 3-11

What was Jesus writing in the dirt
in the story of the adulterous woman?
Two times it's mentioned.
Was He scribbling "These guys are assholes" in Aramaic?
The name of His
gay lover over and over?
Was He adding up His golf club bar bill?
Ciphering His taxes?
Making a grocery list?
Scratching the first line to a spring love poem
before He forgot it?

When they came to Him and said,
'Here is this
woman, this whore,
this adulteress,
what shall we do?", trying
to trap Him so they could turn him in,
was He buying time
while He thought of an answer?
Etching out a mathematical
equation in the dust?
Calculating just how many stones
it would take to kill her?

What was He recording that no one else
wrote it down,
that Simon Peter didn't look over His shoulder to read,
Judas to ponder,

rush to the spot later
for some important message
after He had left the temple?

And the woman, that whore,
that trapped adulteress,
did she care what he was writing?
Was she curious?
When He held her life in His hands
and shamed them off,
what did she see in the dirt
before He sent her away
to sin no more?

The Poet and You, the Locked Man

She lies in bed beside you, the same face, hair, and eyes.
Only the voice is different, the real one gone underground, seething
waiting to explode like a fissure filled with oil.
She blames herself, you blame her.
She is the magnet that attracted the change, the rearrangement
that fell like the straw on the camel's back,
splintered and halved like a toy you used to own
but never played with, broken.
It came like a phone call in the night but softer, an angry whisper
blurred like some photograph of a man you made her throw away.
It came unnoticed, with no pinpoint.
Suddenly the I-love-you's were hollow,
all those promises broken.
She played the music you hated
whenever you were gone, saved the saddest songs
for when you were there.

Slave Story

The way we would do it was
we would each take five aspirins first
so it wouldn't hurt,
then Svetlana would be with some of them for three hours,
and so would I except with others.
Then we would switch until morning.

There were usually two rooms, and
we never fought over them
though we would describe them to one another later.

No matter that one day
I would have my
own bathroom with the men
urinating into a deep toilet
while she had just a bowl of dirty water
and a balcony the men pissed off of
into an abandoned courtyard.

No matter because the whole scene might be switched tomorrow—her
with even a slightly dripping shower, me
with nothing, not even a window while they grunted—
especially when they were drunk—
grunt grunt grunt and then
a dead piglet between my legs before
it had even squealed, and I would
have to wait until it revived again, until
grunt grunt grunt
he called out "Mother!" in his madness
while the others looked on.

I didn't mind when Svetlana would get
the better room.
No matter as long as
she was there.

Diagnosis, Twenty-Five Years Later

Looking back now, it's clear
I had problems.
It's embarrassing too,
my talking and laughing with that metaphorical
lettuce in my teeth, that memorable public
fart in the room, the invisible
dog shit on my shoe while everyone
sniffed the air and said,
Is it her?

O yes, it was me all right;
Don't you remember?

For years I've claimed my roundness
brought the edges out in others,
but I see I relied
on being empty, in fact
depended on it.

Then, anyway.
At that time.

There,
in the drink room,
on the stone porch,
out on the lawn:
the girl they call A Gosling Swimming With Sharks
plays croquet while A Predatory Homosexual, A Failed Composer,
A Poet Going Blind, and a woman who calls herself
A Nigger Fucker, the only one of them who is real,

flip through magazines around the pool.

I am The One Who Will Never Make It,
a textbook example of Narcissistic
Personality Disorder with OCD complications
who, because of obvious reasons,
can't stand her ground.

Remains

Lately I have been staring into the mirror with the blurred gaze of an alcoholic seeing for the first time the way she leers and drools. The man I love is tending his vegetables somewhere behind my eyes. I am doing the dishes. My stomach is bloated with child. While my husband is not the father, we have learned to start forgetting, if not forgiving.

We live in an old trailer on the beach. Children come, ask me for food and water. They would starve, I fear, if it were not for the bread and eggs I hide in the bushes by the gate where they can find them at night. Skinny, worm-ridden, they watch me with somber eyes from the road while my husband says they are like dogs—I must not feed them.

A strange new smell comes up from the southern shore. My husband says the cities are burning. To me, it smells sweet, like mornings when water heats on the stove and I have time enough to sit on the back steps, hugging my knees to my chest, counting the bees that have returned. I saw twelve this morning, buzzing around the tree by the back door.

I love music, but there are no instruments. Once, I had many opportunities to play. Sometimes I stand in the bath, sing softly to myself, listening to a sound so loud, so clear in that small room, the notes like liquid crystals. I am often embarrassed when I sing, often glance uneasily into corners, over my shoulder, always sure someone is listening.

These humid afternoons are void of all movement—even the trees are silent! I pace the yard, fanning sweat from my face and neck. I used to ride on these still days. With the swiftness of my horse against the sky, I was the wind. Last week, they took away our horses. Behind the curtained window, I watched my mare led up the lane in the heat.

Tomorrow morning, when everyone is gone, I will bake bread, collect eggs from where the hens laid. There has been no corn to feed them for some time now. They peck feebly at the dust, toss their heads back, scratch at the dried earth. When my son stirs inside me during the night, I wake and think of them, listless. If there are not enough eggs, I cannot steal without being noticed. I would be intently watched. The children would go hungry.

Salt Fork

The only place I felt I belonged was Ohio;
everyone was fat there.
People weren't ashamed
when they left their towels
to lumber down to the water's brown edge.
They circled their soda cans neatly
in the sand around them
when they were done,
instead of tossing them aside
to be ugly or stepped on.

They even saved their cigarette butts
in neat little piles,
or lined them up parallel in the sand,
like empties for the trash.

No one bothered the red winged black birds
or threw stones at the geese because of their droppings.
The sores on my thighs healed in that sun,
and though the doctor had said
I couldn't go in the water,
it seemed so beautiful,
the yellow air full of dragon flies.

Even my fear melted among them.
I dreamed Peter loved me again there,
that what he had once called
a mud hole with dirty sand
was now a sparkling resort,

clear, cold glacier water,
an enthusiastic lake with a mountain view,
where none of the bathers had tattoos.
He rolled across my boney hip and said,
Your body is lovely.
He sucked my aureole and whispered,
Your body is mine.

Shrieks, whistles, a thudding ball,
the flat beeping of surgery equipment,
and I awoke on that wide towel, hearing a round
mother telling her plump son,
Don't be afraid, honey, this is Ohio sand.
It's brown, but it washes off.

I Never Think of You

I never think of you but when
I am asked by a man to explain myself,
and then it is always that same sky,
and the buildings seeming distant under it,
as if you and I again were poised
alone on the edge of a desert,
the tooting horns of a reduced street irrelevant,
of another world.

Until then I had never understood mauve:
twilight in the department store,
on a woman's eyelids,
the fresh expression of this
new season of self-expression:

     Imitate
Imitate.

More orange than the dusk through which it passed,
sweeter than the faint
bruises on a thigh, the color
of that sky while the Wedding—
we must not forget the Wedding!—
Reception carried on inside:
you, the eager guest,
I, the missing bride.

Anwar Sadat's Wife's Lover

Though he is dying,
there is laughter in the house.
There is good food,
wine,
existential jokes.
There is politeness,
the occasional flash of anger because
like the current politics
this is not fair.

His face has become
a baked
calavera with bulging eyes
and a sincere grin.
One look and I know
I will visit him again
before it is over.
I think of 1000 count sheets
and bed sores.
I want to tell his wife, but I wait.

Though he is dying,
there is plenty of time.
I surrender myself to its current
as they obviously have done
in spite of his protests—
I feel stronger today!

Of course he does.
He is losing his gravity,

bit by bit becoming lighter in the investment,
though still heavy in body,
though lighter in body than before.

He dreams he becomes Anwar Sadat's wife's lover.
When they are done, as there is something else he wants
to say, she leaves through a swinging door.
Startled by the noises in the street,
she doesn't hear.

Gleaning

I've been here before,
but I see now
I was sloppy then.
There's still plenty to pick up,
plenty left behind,
so much I must have been full
when I first passed by.

How long ago was it
I stood at this particular
place, with that specific
rock, in a moment
similar to this,
those brambles
way on the edge of the field?
Did I know then
where the path was between them?
Or did I scratch through,
push with my head down,
arms loaded?

Perhaps I left so much behind
because I thought
there would always be more up ahead,
yet here I am again,
looking eagerly for a few lumps of
sweetness that have
survived the heat and rains
since then,

that haven't molded
been picked apart by birds,
scrounged by stray cattle,
or kicked up by playing children.
There is still sufficient
for today's purposes.
The next time I'm here
I know
I will be searching for grains.

Praying for Pol Pot

Doolin wouldn't do it.
He rushed from the room,
lit a cigarette,
though smoking was forbidden.

In the hall, the bishop asked him what was wrong,
why he wasn't back inside
learning how to pray better
with the others.

That son of a bitch asked me to pray for Pol Pot! Doolin railed
and jerked his head back toward the open door
like he had been grabbed from behind
by the collar.

Look, said Doolin. *I don't feel* sorry *because Joseph's
drunken father beat him with a stick of firewood!*
The ones he had left behind could hear.
I don't give a shit *that poor Adolf didn't become an artist!*

He pinched the brown filter
trembling between his fingers and by habit
blew smoke dragon-like from his nostrils.
The bishop merely nodded.

That afternoon, the fresh-faced priest was removed
from his position as Retreat Coordinator.
A stubbled old man took his place,
someone Doolin had known from Cambodia,

the one that baptized him
after that terrible spring,
after that month of rain in Phnom Penh
when Doolin's friends floated in the ditches.

For Cho Seung-hui

Walking

You take each step with a strength I cannot begin to feel,
the lifting, swinging of your total body
suspended inside the heavy braces you say sometimes abhor you, frighten you
like a man unable to stop his own dream.
I stand behind you, helpless except to guide,
support your fall and break it,
a split rain fence coming between a falling oak
and the ground.
The steps drop off behind us, a well yawning and open,
drawing us dangerously back down to the landing,
the dark, shadowed stairs at the bottom.
You resist and climb. I follow.
My fingers looped in the back of your jeans
give me the illusion that I am helping.
It's up to you to make the curbs, feel your way
with unfeeling toes along the relentless sidewalks,
the uneven mounds of dirt left by lawn mowers.
I've watched you from the Day Room, out on the hospital lawn,
your strolling plant and swing, plant and swing,
no one to stop when you pitch, drop the crutches,
tumble forward onto the dry grass alone.

His Mother's Love

He was hers first,
her vessel, and she
wore him down as a woman
scrapes the bottom of a burned pot,
knowing her husband is with someone else,
someone he works with,
someone who inhabits that cold, secret world
of the operating room,
someone who doesn't shrink
when the entrails are exposed
like she does.

Except he is her son.
Except the burned pot is not aluminum
but steel.
Except there is no single bulb from a wire
dangling drearily above that stove
where she stands, then leans, and scrapes.

Instead, the light is porcelain,
Chinese,
a dragon,
the third one she has tried in that corner.

Where did the other two lamps go?
To his house
each time she redecorated.
As you can guess
lamps come to him still and will
as long as she's alive,
until all his rooms are filled with artificial light,
and he's forever marked
by her small spoon.

Your Letters Still Lie on My Dresser

Your letters still lie on my dresser, the foreign postmarks
hieroglyphics so ancient they cannot be deciphered
or worse, translated with a meaning unclear,
hazy like the fog drifting off the pines,
heat and water into smoke.
I bet on them,
cling to them, an adult
to fairy tales, the woman in the desert
who sees a mirage galloping toward her
and sits in the hot sand
waiting for it.
I wake from dreams and fight to sleep,
to re-enter the domain where we still exist,
where the great vine trees of the jungle are still old men
rocking back and forth,
swaying in imperceptible circles,
bewitching me with their secrets,
their great moans until I must follow their deep
guttural groans through the menacing greenness,
and I stand at their feet looking upward,
eyes wide and mouth open, an enchanted child, rooted.
Then you always come for me, a brilliant bird,
lead me with your arm to our tent by the river
long before darkness begins to stalk the thin paths,
threatening the air with a machete.

Turning Inside Out

I would do if I could,
turn my eyes inward yet keep
that other half still

unknown to me, my constant companion,
just the distance of skin away,
but this time on the outside,

glistening into the dry air,
a steaming colander of
hot, red organs,

pushed with their membranes
from one universe
into another.

Meanwhile, now on the inside,
nice and dark though somewhat
suffocated and thoroughly,

gratefully, unable to see,
I remember the world—
glowing—the way my arms

and legs moved me through space,
how I orbited other
bodies, other spheres, other

more complicated shapes.
The blackness is anaerobic now.
Air would kill me.

SANDRA KOLANKIEWICZ has a BA and PhD from Ohio University and attended the Writing Seminars at Johns Hopkins. Her collection of stories *Con/sequential Monologues* was a finalist for the 2007 Spokane Prize, the 2007 Tartt's First Prize, the 2008 Hudson Prize, and the 2008 and 2009 G.S. Sharat Chandra Prize for short fiction at BkMk Press. Her collection entitled *Isla* was a finalist for the 2007 Hudson Prize and the 2008 St. Lawrence Prize. Her novel *Blue Eyes Don't Cry* won the 2008 Hackney Award for the novel from Birmingham Southern and was a finalist for the 2008 George Garrett Prize from Texas Review Press. She currently teaches English at West Virginia University Parkersburg and is active in the autism recovery community.